W9-BDB-776

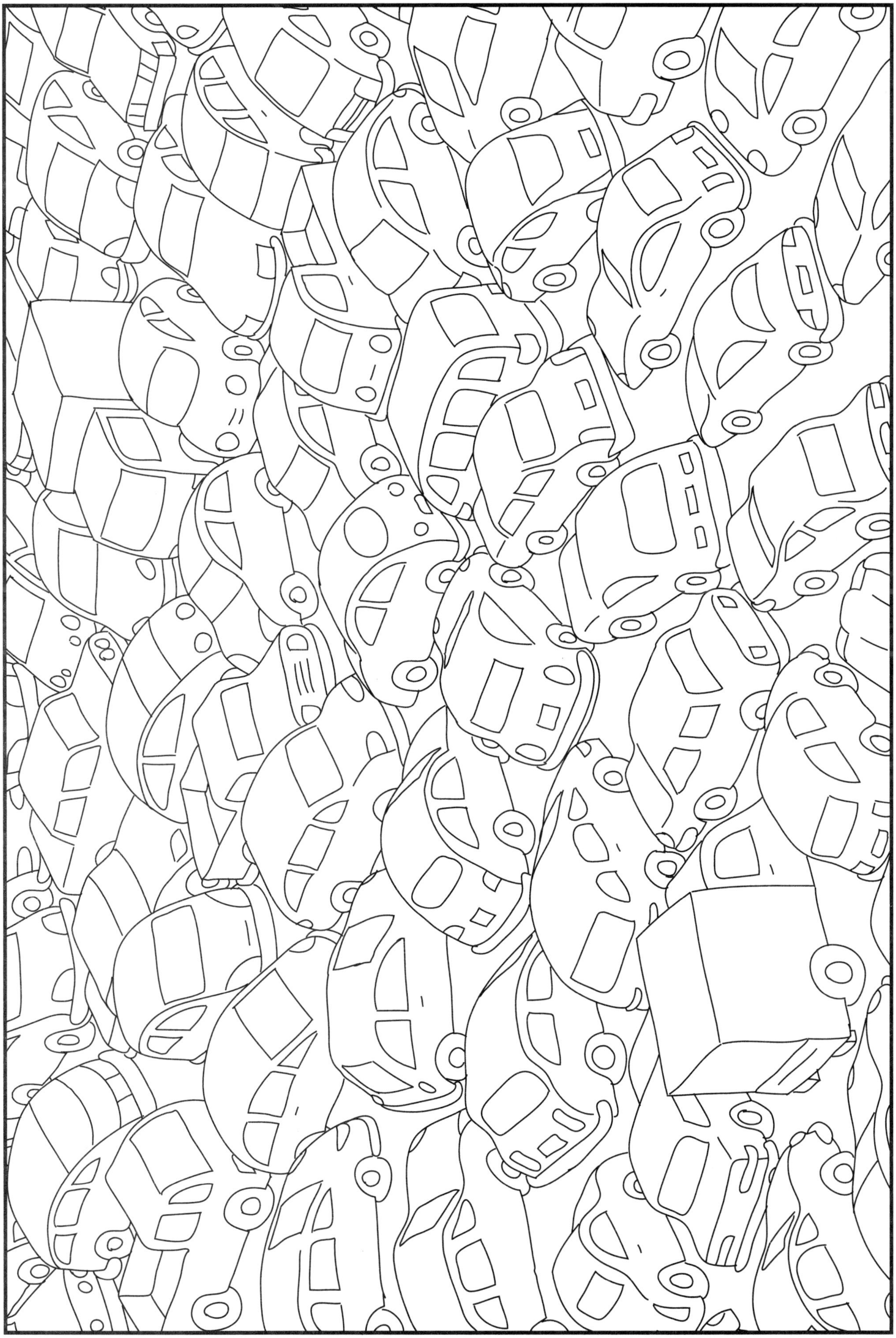

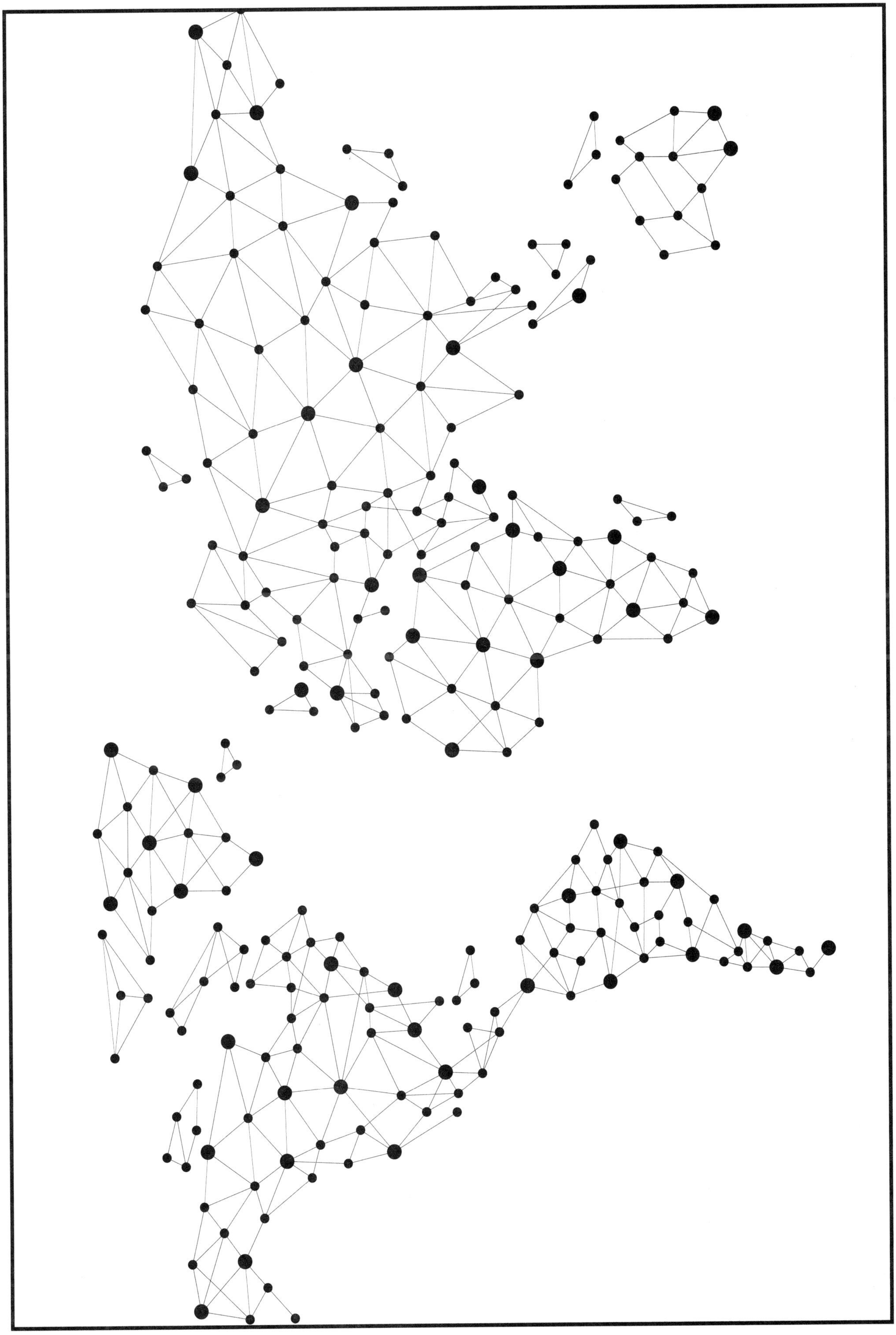

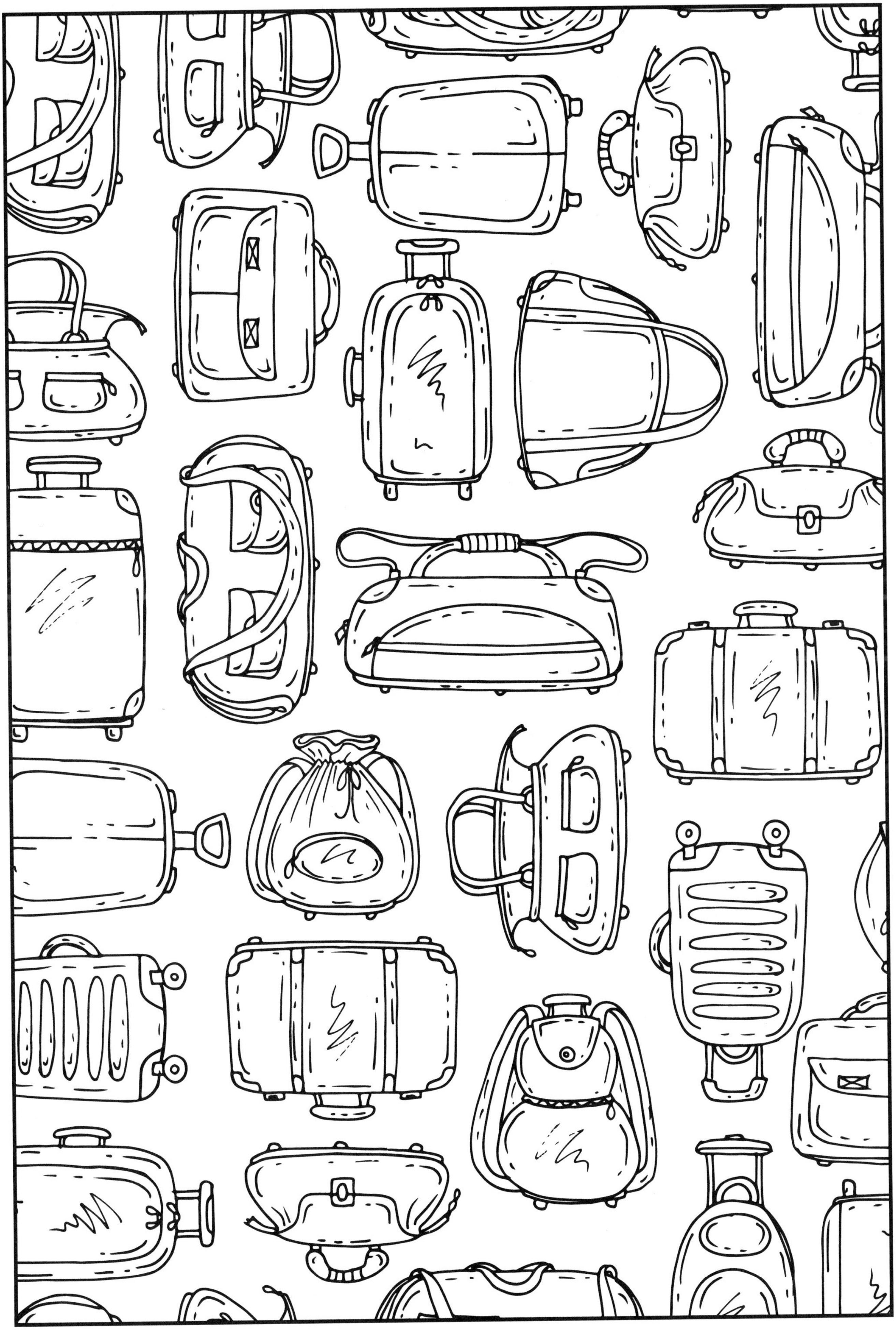

HI!

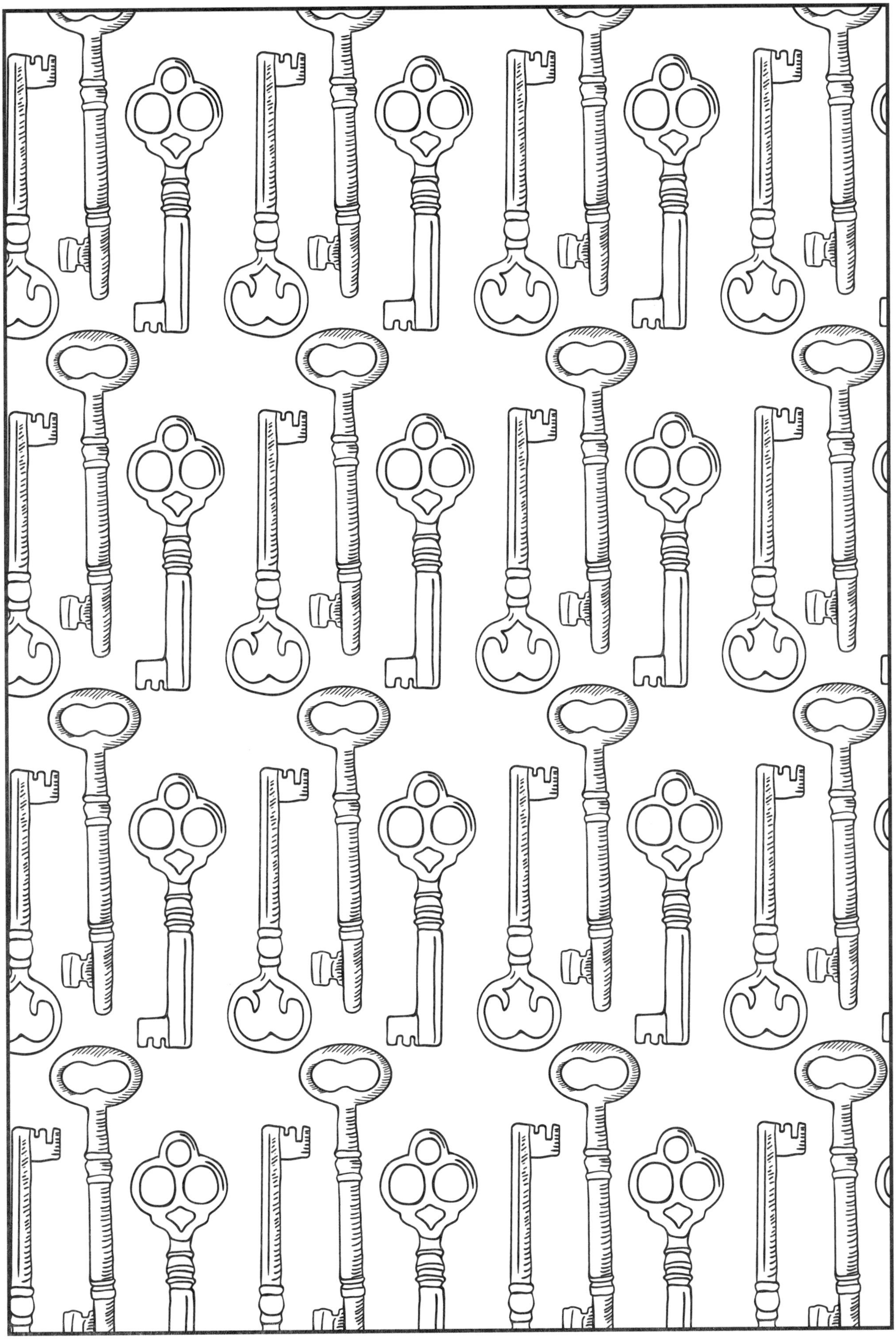

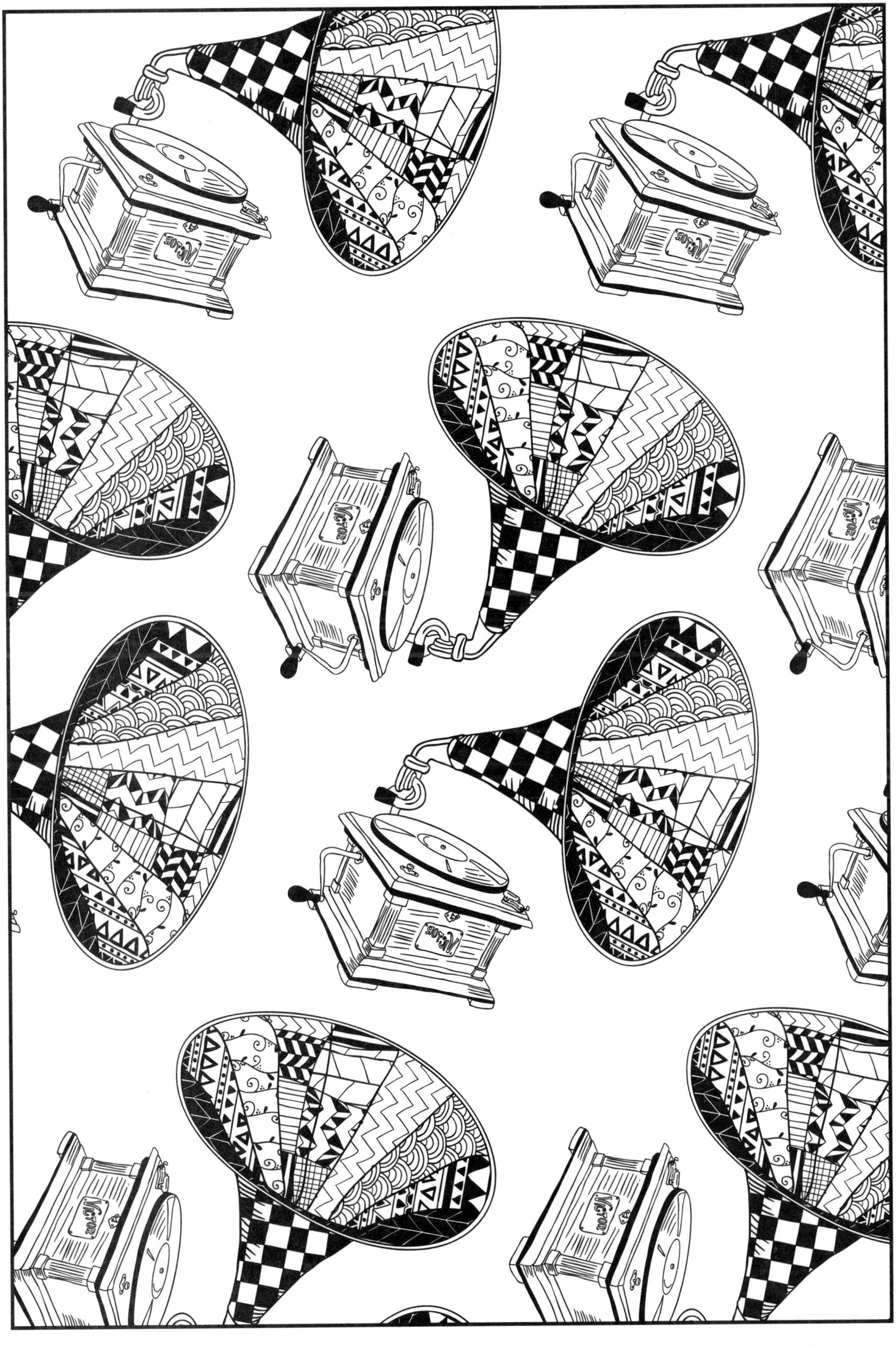
Victor

MENU
20
PASS

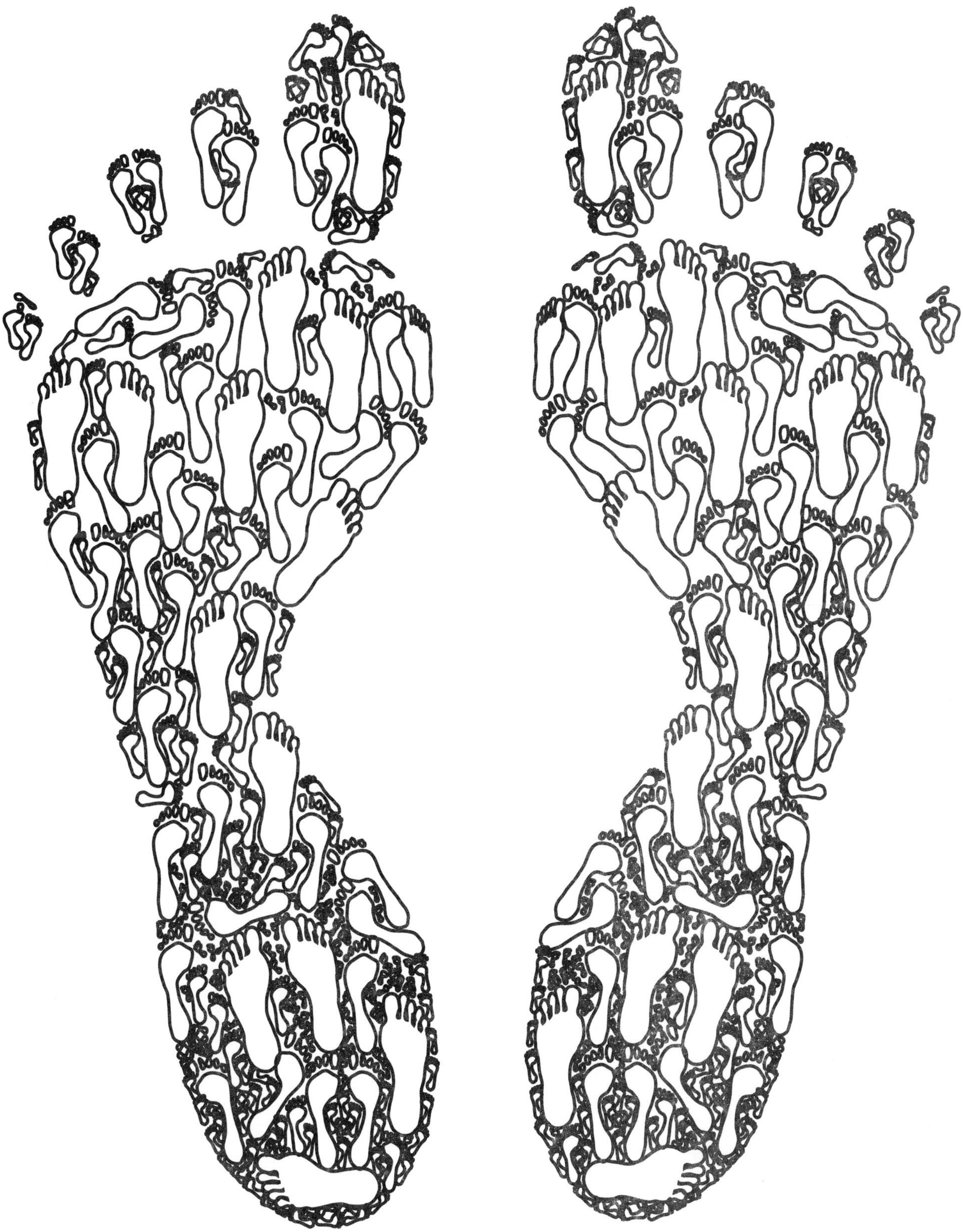

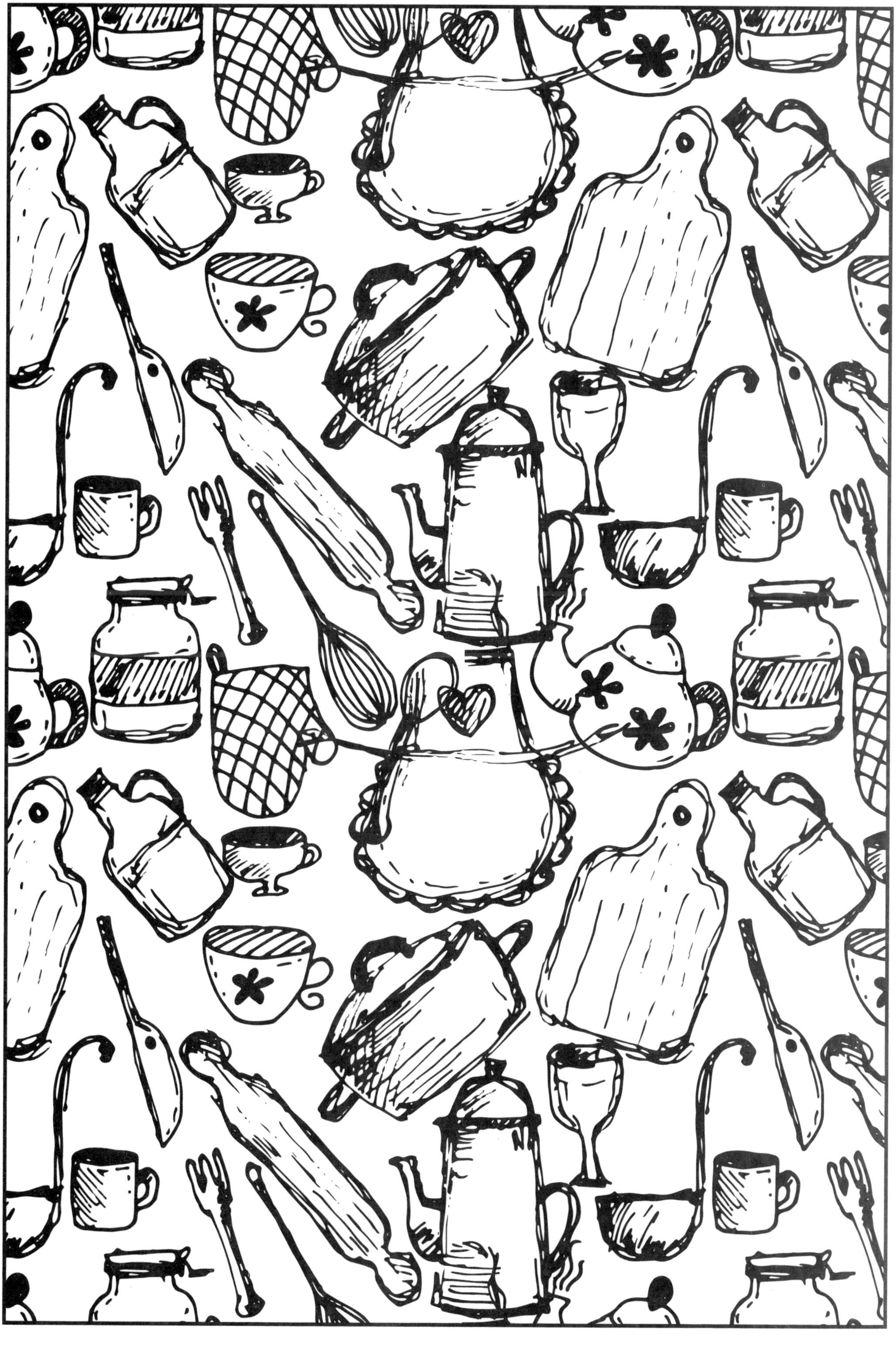

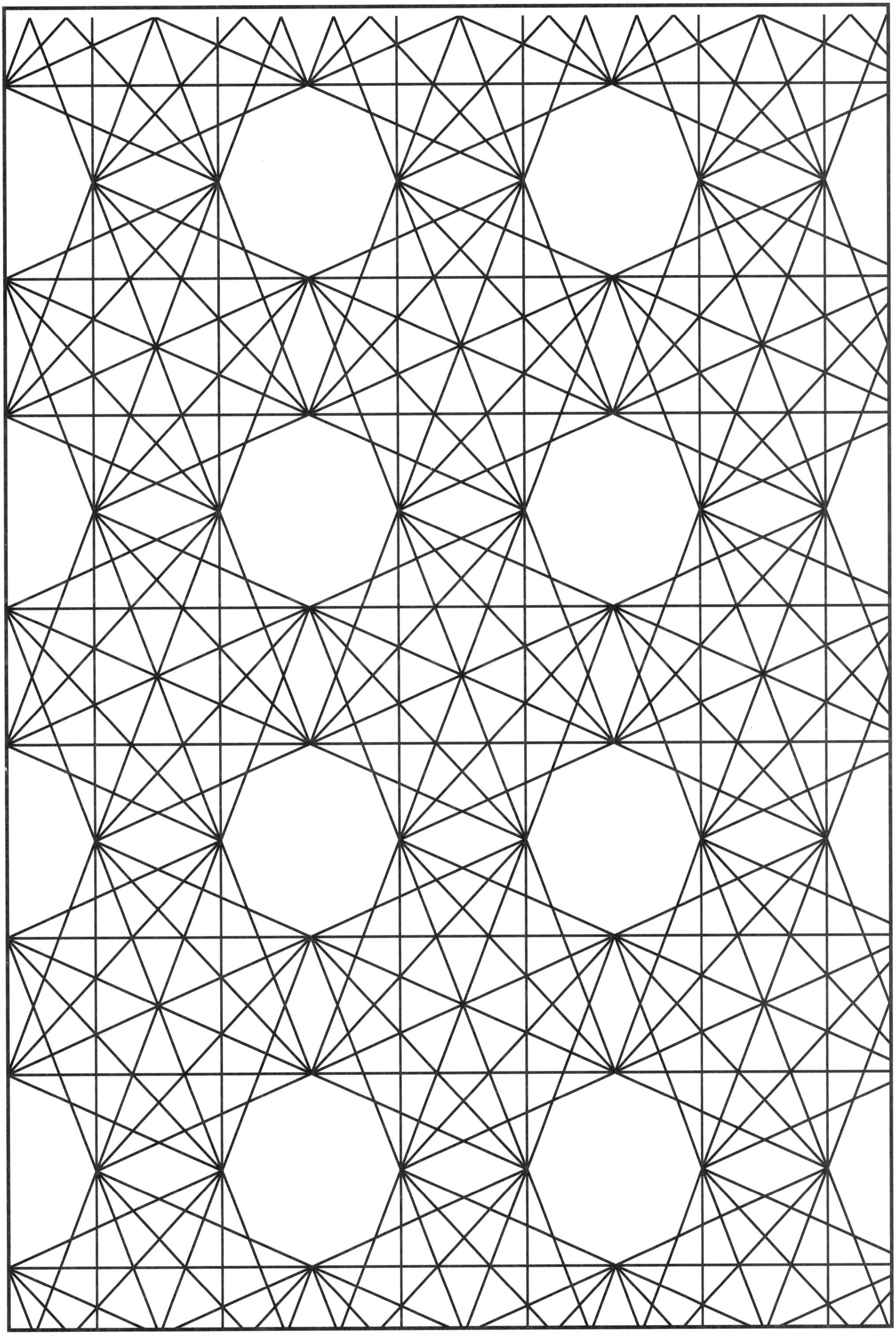

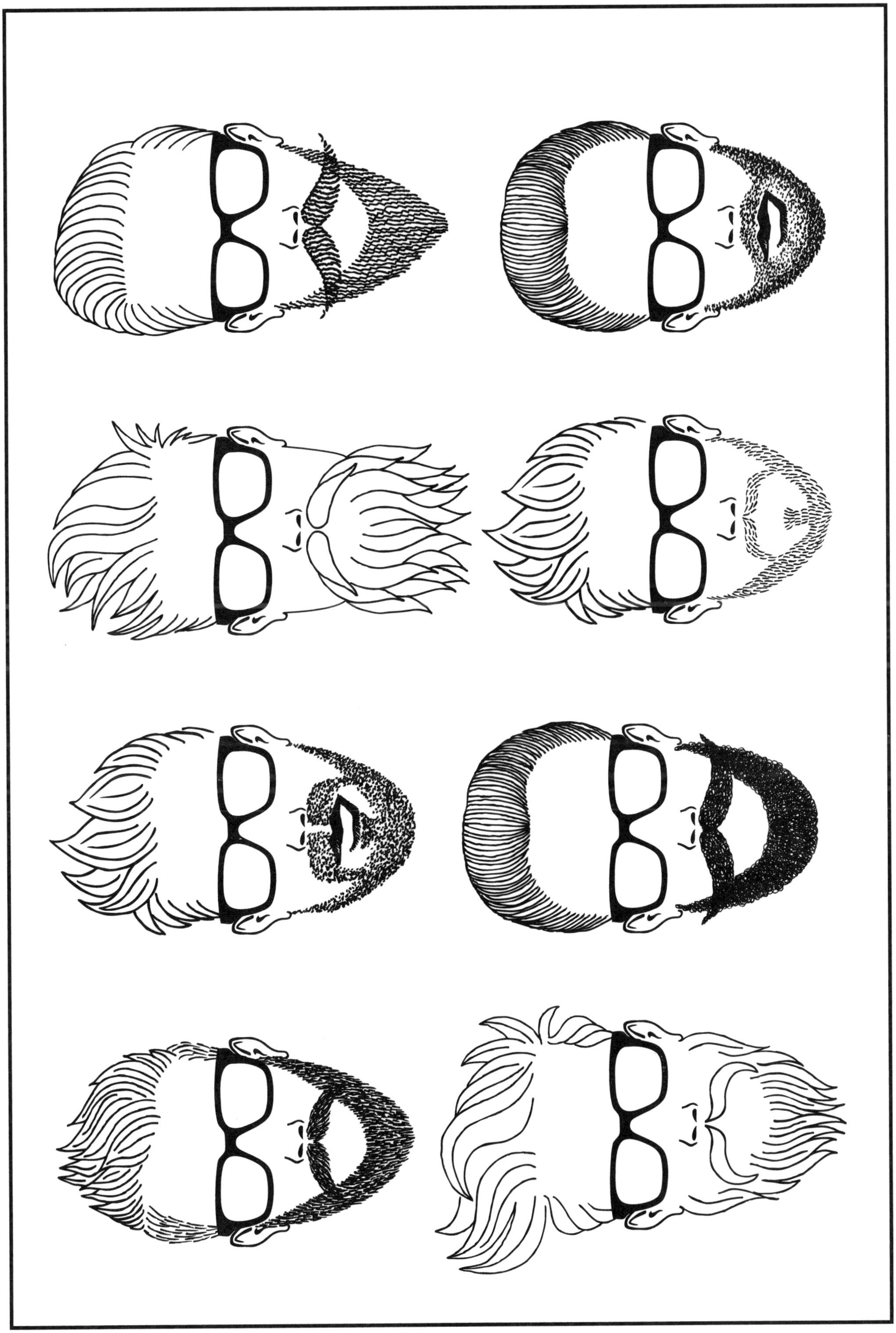

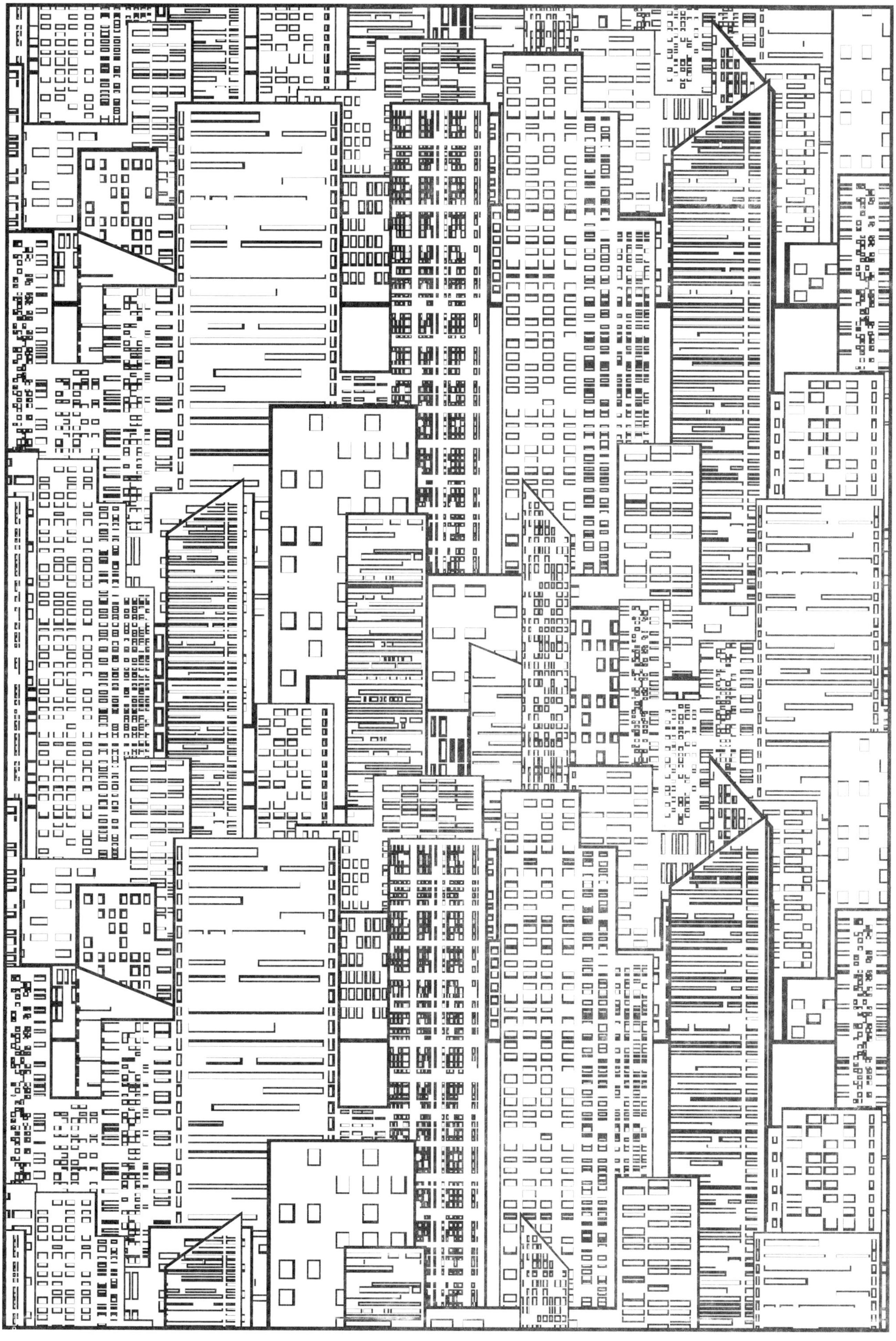